Nadja Knab-Leers • Heike Roland • Stefanie Thomas

Sew Scandinavian

55 fabulous projects for the home

SEARCH PRESS

Contents

—⋘⋙—

Are you looking for ideas that will add a welcoming touch to your home? If so, the useful and attractive items in this chapter will inspire you to decorate your hallway with pretty accessories.

—⋘⋙—

In this chapter we will show you how you can transform your dining table into one that is lovingly laid using fresh designs and ideas. A few pretty decorations will make your dining room and lounge feel really cosy.

—⋘⋙—

Everyone wants to feel safe and sound at home within their own four walls. The bathroom, bedroom and study are places of refuge. You will find countless ideas here to transform them into real retreats.

—⋘⋙—

Here you will find explanations of frequently used techniques, helpful hints and tips, and patterns to help you make the items in the book.

—⋘⋙—

Sew Scandinavian

55 fabulous projects for the home

Welcome to Scandinavia

Welcome to Scandinavia! We are delighted to invite you to share our love of cheerful patterns, fresh colours and simple, Scandinavian design.
We have made it our mission to dream up beautiful objects for you and your home.

We are sure you have all known the pride and happiness that can come from holding something in your hands that you have made yourself. These feelings have aroused in us a real passion for making attractive objects, and what better place to make them for than our own homes? This is where we can turn our ideas into reality, give our creativity free rein and make the space in which we live our own.

Decorations and pretty everyday objects not only make our daily lives more pleasant and comfortable, but also give our homes an individual touch.
We hope that with this book we can inspire you to create a beautiful and welcoming home of your own – in true Scandinavian style!
Have fun and 'ha det så kul'!

A Warm Welcome

The hallway is the threshold between the outside world and our own living space. When we go out, we get ready in the hall, whether we are going for a walk, going to work or visiting friends. And this is where we are warmly greeted when we come home again and, of course, where we welcome our guests too. It is therefore well worth giving this area our attention by preparing a warm welcome for ourselves and others.

Everything in Its Place

Lampshade

Lampshade, Ø 25cm (9¾in) • Floral fabric in grey, 15cm (6in) • Dotted fabric in grey, 10cm (4in) • Ricrac braid in pink, 1.7m (67in) • Satin ribbon in grey, 2m (78¾in) • Woven interfacing, e.g. G700, 30cm (11¾in) • Double-sided adhesive web, e.g. Vliesofix, 20cm (7¾in) • Textile adhesive

Cut a 13cm-wide (5in) strip from the floral fabric and the woven interfacing and a 7cm-wide (2¾in) strip from the double-sided adhesive web. The lengths will be the same as the circumference of the shade, plus a 3cm (1¼in) seam allowance.

Attach the woven interfacing to the reverse of the floral fabric, then iron a 1cm (½in) turning to the reverse of the fabric along the long edges and one narrow edge. Line up the double-sided adhesive web with the reverse of the dotted fabric, cut out and attach it to the centre of the floral strip.

Place the completed strip tightly around the shade and attach the short sides to one another using textile adhesive. Attach ricrac braid and ten satin bows.

Key holder

Plywood, 6mm (¼in) thick, 40 x 40cm (15¾ x 15¾in) • Dotted fabric in grey, 50cm (19¾in) • Fabric remnant in pink decorated with ladies and dogs • Satin ribbon in pink/brown, 6mm (¼in) wide, 2m (78¾in) • Decorative braid in brown and pink • Double-sided adhesive web, e.g. Vliesofix, 50cm (19¾in) • Six offset wood screws, Ø 2.3mm (⅛in), 2cm (¾in) long • Two picture rings • Textile adhesive • Hammer and small nail • Patterns on page 78 and sheet B

Saw out the shape of the wooden heart, then attach the dotted fabric using double-sided adhesive web (see page 66). Next, attach five small hearts and one medium-sized heart to the large heart using motifs from the fabric remnant. Preferably use double-sided adhesive web for this and make sure that the hearts are evenly spaced.

Glue satin ribbon around the edge of the heart and to the reverse of the picture rings. Now you can screw in the offset screws and decorate the hearts with small bows.

To make it easier: use the hammer and nail to bore little holes in advance. That way the offset screws will screw into the board more easily.

Large bag

Wool felt in pink, 2, 50 x 50cm (19¾ x 19¾ in)
• Dotted fabric in grey, 2, 50 x 50cm (19¾ x 19¾ in)
• Floral fabric in grey/pink, 2, 30 x 50cm (11¾ x 19¾in)
• Fabric in pink with ladies and dogs, 20 x 20cm (7¾ x 7¾in)
• Velvet ribbon in raspberry red, 2.6m (102¼in)
• Ruched ribbon in grey check, 80cm (31½ in)
• Woven interfacing, e.g. G700, 2, 50 x 50cm (19¾ x 19¾in)
• Double-sided adhesive web, e.g. Vliesofix,
50cm (19¾ in) • Bag handle for threading • Two glass
beads in pink Ø 2cm (¾ in) • Thirty-two acrylic lozenge beads
in crystal, 2 x 1.4cm (¾ x ½ in) • Pattern sheet B

Cut out the large bag piece twice from wool felt and
woven interfacing and iron the interfacing on to the
reverse. Cut out the lining twice from the dotted
fabric. Now make up bag piece 2 twice in floral
fabric with double-sided adhesive web on the
reverse, as described on page 66, and attach the
fabric heart to one of these pieces, again with
double-sided adhesive web. Iron both the floral
pieces to the wool felt pieces.

Sew the ruched ribbon around the heart – it is best
to start at the tip and turn in the ends. Sew the
velvet ribbon on to the top edge of the floral fabric.

Sew the wool felt pieces to the straight edge of the
dotted fabric pieces (lining) right sides together, then
sew each of the wool felt pieces and the lining pieces
together, right sides facing, leaving a 15cm (6in)
opening along the bottom edge of the lining for
turning out. After turning out, iron the seams flat and
close up the lining.

Thread the beads on to the handles: eight lozenge
beads and one glass bead and then another eight
lozenge beads for each handle. Place the handles in
the centre about 1cm (½in) below the top edge of
the bag and mark the positions with tailor's chalk.

Feed four 40cm-long (15¾in) pieces of velvet ribbon
through the handle rings. Fold the ribbons in half
and sew just beneath the ring on the marking.
Finally, tie the ends of the ribbons into bows and
then the bag is ready.

Bag pendant

Bag-size karabiner clip
- Ricrac braid in pink, 30cm (11¾in)
- Grey leather, 10 x 10cm (4 x 4in)

Attach a fabric motif using double-sided adhesive web to the wool felt and cut it into the shape of a heart following the pattern on page 78.

Glue the ruched ribbon on to the reverse of the heart and glue ricrac braid on to the front. Thread a piece of ribbon 18cm (7in) long through the karabiner clip. Attach the ends to the reverse of the heart and cover it all with a leather heart. Finally, sew on a bow in velvet ribbon.

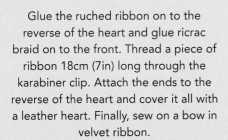

Small bag

Fabric in pink with ladies and dogs, 25 x 25cm (9¾ x 9¾in)
- Dotted fabric in grey, 25 x 25cm (9¾ x 9¾in) • Double-sided adhesive volume fleece, e.g. HH650, 25 x 25cm (9¾ x 9¾in) • Ruched ribbon in grey check, 80cm (31½in) • Ricrac braid in pink, 80cm (31½in) • Satin ribbon in pink, 50cm (19¾in) • Wooden beads in pink, 10 x Ø 1cm (½in) and 7 x Ø 1.5cm (⅝in) • Pattern sheet A

Cut out the heart twice from both fabrics and from the fleece with a 1cm (½in) seam allowance. Iron two different fabric hearts together with the fleece in between.

Neaten the hearts with zigzag stitch and stitch first the ruched ribbon and then the ricrac braid around the front.

Now attach the beads to the satin ribbon as shown and knot it in between each one. Leave 2.5cm (1in) at the ends. Finally, place the ends against the markings on either side of the opening and sew the hearts to one another, leaving the opening free.

Clothes hooks

Plywood, 1cm (½ in) thick, 50 x 25cm (19¾ x 9¾ in)
• Decorative metal clothes hooks in white • Acrylic paint in white and red
• Four short screws • Screwdriver (suitable for the screws) • Sandpaper
• Patterns on pages 69 and 70

Saw out the shape of the wooden hearts and smooth the edges using sandpaper. Paint the hearts wet-on-wet with the acrylic paint. When dry, drill the holes into the wood for the clothes hooks and screw on the hooks.

To make it easier: do you want to attach the hooks to the wall? If so, transfer the holes on the hearts to the wall and insert rawlplugs. Attach the metal hooks with long screws right through the heart directly into the wall.

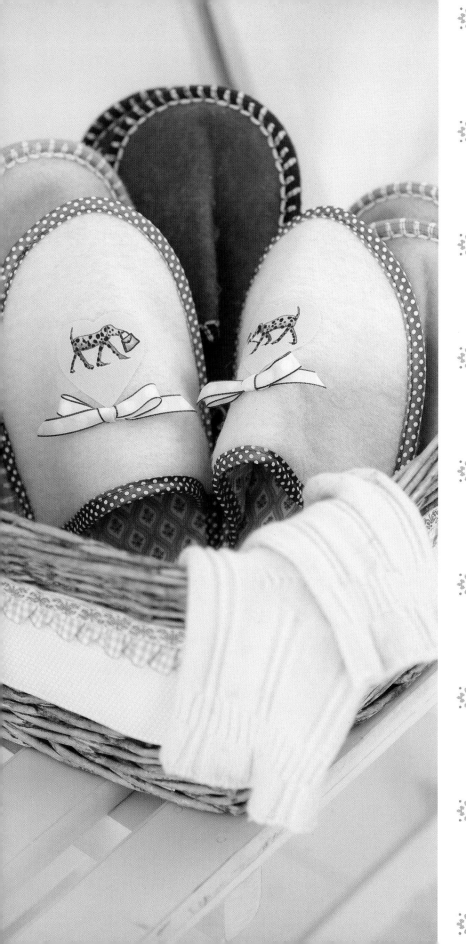

Slippers

Wool felt in pink, 40cm (15¾ in)
• Floral fabric in grey/pink, 40cm (15¾ in)
• Fabric remnant in pink with ladies and dogs
• Decorative ribbon in pink/brown, 50cm
(19¾ in) • Folded bias binding in spotted
pink, 2m (78¾ in) • Double-sided adhesive
web, e.g. Vliesofix, 50cm (19¾ in) • Double-
sided adhesive volume fleece, e.g. HH650, 40cm
(15¾ in) • Patterns on page 78 and sheet B

Cut out the pieces for the shoe twice
from the wool felt, the floral fabric and
the volume fleece. Now place a
matching piece of fleece between the
wool felt and the floral fabric and secure
the layers of fabric together by ironing.
Sew around all the edges, keeping close
to the edge.

※

Using double-sided adhesive web (see
page 66), decorate the fronts with two
hearts from the motif fabric and then
finish the straight edge with bias
binding, ironing the binding in half
beforehand. Now place the upper pieces
against the soles, so that the floral fabric
is against the floral fabric.

※

Edge the whole outer edge with bias
binding. Turn the ends of the binding in
by 1cm (½in) to make it look neater.
Finally, decorate each heart with
a bow. Finished!

To make it easier: if your feet are larger or
smaller, you can make the soles a little larger or
smaller at the end — or use ready-made felt
slippers in your size and simply decorate them
with fabric hearts and bias binding.

Shoe basket

Basket in grey, 30 x 30cm (11¾ x 11¾in)
- Dotted fabric in pink, 50cm (19¾in)
- Decorative braid in dark pink/light pink, 1.5m (59in)
- Elastic ruched ribbon in grey check, 1.2m (47¼in)

Measure the circumference of the basket, allowing a 2cm (¾in) seam allowance, and cut a strip from the dotted fabric 16cm (6¼in) wide and of the required length. Sew along the length of the strip following the width of the sewing machine foot to form a tube, turn out and iron.

Now turn in one of the open ends approximately 1cm (½in). Push the opposite end 1cm (½in) into the pre-ironed opening and topstitch close to the edge, so that the fabric forms a closed ring.

Topstitch the lower long edge, keeping close to the edge, and decorate the top edge with ruched ribbon and decorative braid. Stretch the ribbon/braid so that the fabric cuff sits closely on the basket. Finally, sew on a little bow by hand and pull the finished cuff over the basket.

To make it even nicer: if you want to have an attractive lining for your basket, you could make this from the dotted fabric and volume fleece, for example. Simply measure the base of the basket and cut out a shape twice from the fabric and once from the volume fleece, e.g. H640. Attach the two pieces of fabric together with the fleece in between and neaten the edges with narrow zigzag stitch.

The instructions for the teddy are on page 57.

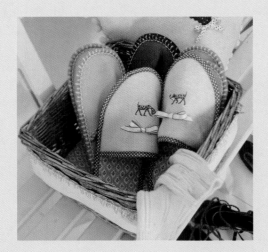

Four Little Mice

Mouse

Cotton fabric in white, 15cm (6in)
• Cotton fabric in patterned pink/red or blue, 15cm (6in)
• Rocaille beads in black, 2 x Ø 2mm (⅛in) and 1 x Ø 4mm
(¼ in) • Cotton ribbon in white, 15cm (6in) • Wadding
• Granules • Strong sewing thread in black • Patterns on
pages 68 and 69

First, cut out all pieces of fabric according to the
pattern. Cut out the slits for the little ears where
marked. Now sew together one patterned and one
white ear, right sides together, as far as the opening for
turning and turn out.

✳

Wrap the corners of the ears towards the centre and
secure inside the seam allowance. Sew the ears into the
slits left for them. To do this, place the edges of both
slits right sides together, place the ear in between and
sew both edges together, making sure that the
patterned ear pieces point in the direction of the nose.

✳

Next, sew the head and body pieces right sides
together to form a single piece. Place this piece right
sides together along the fabric fold line and close the
straight edge with a seam. Match the right sides
together for the base and sew both pieces together as
far as the opening for turning. Catch in the cotton-
ribbon tail where marked.

✳

Turn your mouse out and stuff with wadding and
granules. Close the opening for turning with mattress
stitch. Sew on the rocaille beads for the eyes and nose,
pull the strong threads through to form whiskers and
knot the ends of both threads together to secure in
place. Hold the wadding in place in the head with a few
stitches so that it does not slip down.

A hare with a heart

Cotton fabric in blue and brown, 15cm (6in) each ● Cotton fabric remnants in white, and blue and white check ● Volume fleece, e.g. H630, 15cm (6in) ● Embroidery thread in black, orange and green ● Pompom in white, Ø 1cm (½in) ● Flower buttons, five white and one light blue ● Wooden carrot button ● White wire, 2 x 5cm (2in) and 3 x 15cm (6in) ● Wadding ● Pattern on page 71

Cut out all the pieces according to the pattern, making sure that the heart made from volume fleece is cut without a seam allowance. Iron the fleece piece on to the reverse of the corresponding piece of fabric.

❋

Place the fabric pieces for the head, arms, legs, ears and heart right sides together and sew up as far as the opening for turning. With the head, also leave openings for the base of the ears. Turn out the individual pieces and close the opening for the heart using mattress stitch. Lightly stuff the other pieces with wadding and sew together the openings inside the seam allowance, so that nothing can slip out.

❋

Push the ears into the head openings and close up using mattress stitch. Embroider on the eyes and the mouth and attach the pompom. Thread the two short pieces of wire through the face as in the picture. It is worth piercing the holes first in the correct places using a thicker needle.

❋

Sew both body pieces together right sides facing as far as the opening for turning, incorporating the arms and legs where marked. Turn the body out and close up the opening using mattress stitch. Now you can attach the head to the body using a few stitches.

❋

To hang up, thread a long piece of wire through the ears and twist the ends of the wires into a ring. You can make the hare look more appealing by bending one ear forwards. Now embroider the heart and decorate with buttons; it can then be attached to the hare using the remaining pieces of wire.

❋

Sew the light blue button on to the neckerchief and the carrot to one of the hands. Finally, fray the neckerchief a little along the straight edges and tie.

Little
Master Hare

Bon Appetit!

Mealtimes are a chance for everyone to get together. When the whole family is sitting around the dining table, it is one of the happiest, most fun places to be. Often everyone will retire afterwards to the living room or the garden to continue their discussions. Whether indoors or out, you can turn the heart of your home into a cosy living space with a few carefully chosen decorations. We hope you will have great get-togethers — bon appetit!

Egg cosies

Cotton fabric in white, 15cm (6in) • Patterned cotton fabric remnants in lime green, turquoise or pink • Double-sided adhesive web, e.g. Vliesofix, 30cm (11¾in) • Ricrac braid in pink and white, 30cm (11¾in) each • Matching-coloured decorative braid or satin ribbon, 30cm (11¾in) • Approximately twenty renaissance beads in pink, Ø 4mm (¼in) • Glass-shaped beads in turquoise, Ø 1.2cm (½in) • Textile adhesive • Pattern on page 72

First, using the pattern, prepare the pieces for the front and back and attach them to each other using double-sided adhesive web according to the instructions on page 66, making sure that the large piece of fabric is reinforced with white cotton fabric on the reverse, so that the egg cosy holds its shape.

Glue on the pink-coloured ricrac braid as shown and sew the front and back pieces together down to the lower edge, wrong sides together, using zigzag stitch. Finally, glue white ricrac braid around the opening and decorate the cosy with beads and a bow.

Lanterns

Lantern, Ø 13cm (5in) • Spotted fabric in lime green or pink check, 8 x 87cm (3¼ x 34¼in) • Velvet ribbon in turquoise, 2cm (¾in) wide, 11cm (4¼in) • Approximately ten renaissance beads in green or pyramid beads in brown, Ø 6mm (¼in) • Glass-shaped beads in pink or turquoise, approximately Ø 1.5cm (⅝in)

Fold the strip in half right sides together and sew the open long edges together 1cm (½in) from the edge, leaving around 4cm (1½in) open at both ends. The finished size is 3 × 87cm (1¼in × 34¼in). Turn the band out, iron and sew the narrow ends to each other 1cm (½in) from the edge and right sides together. Iron the seam allowance open and close up the open places by hand.

For the double bow, fold the fabric ring in half and stitch twice as indicated in the diagram on page 75. Pull the bows apart so that all the seams are lying on top of one another, and sew together in the centre along the seams. Attach the velvet ribbon over the top and sew on the beads.

You can adjust the measurements to any size: for a larger or smaller circumference, you will need to adjust the measurement of the strip of fabric. Take the circumference of the glass and multiply by 2.15 — and adjust the seams for the bow accordingly.

Tablecloth

- *Spotted fabric in lime green, 1.5 x 1.5m (59 x 59in)*
- *Check fabric in pink, 2.1m (82¾in)* • *Ricrac braid in turquoise, 6m (236¼in)*

Neaten the edges of the spotted fabric all the way round using a sewing machine. Cut four 30cm-wide (11¾in) and 2.1m-long (82¾in) strips from the check fabric and iron them in half lengthways, right sides together.

Cut the narrow ends at a 45° angle to form a point and sew together following the width of the sewing machine foot. Sew up the long edges too, but leave 10cm (4in) open for turning.

Turn out the strips, iron and close up by hand. Sew the strips centred along the edges of the tablecloth following the width of the sewing machine foot, leaving approximately 50cm (19¾in) overhanging to the right and the left. Finally, sew on the ricrac braid.

Napkin ring

Wooden napkin ring, Ø 4.5cm (1¾ in) • Check fabric in pink or turquoise, 6 x 39cm (2¼ x 15¼ in) • Patterned cotton fabric in light blue/red, 5 x 9cm (2 x 3½ in) • Glass shaped beads in turquoise or pink, Ø 1.2cm (½ in) • Eleven renaissance beads in dark pink or light pink, Ø 4mm (¼ in) • Pink acrylic paint • Clear varnish • Textile adhesive

First of all, paint and varnish the napkin rings and leave to dry. In the meantime, iron the long edges of the fabric strips together, then iron over to the folded edge, iron together again and iron flat once more.

Open the long strip again, close right sides together at the narrow edges to form a ring and place together again. Now topstitch both strips along the open long edge, keeping close to the edge.

Glue the fabric ring to the napkin ring and make the excess at the end into a double bow (see diagram on page 75), pin in place and secure with adhesive. Now place the short strip around the bow and sew the turned-in ends together by hand. Finally, sew on the beads.

Napkin

Check fabric in pink and turquoise, 40 x 40cm (15¾ x 15¾ in) or remnant • Patterned cotton fabric remnant in light blue/red • Iron-on glitter foil in turquoise • Ricrac braid in pink or light blue, 1.7m (67in) • Heart stamp • Double-sided adhesive web, e.g. Vliesofix • Pattern on page 78

Neaten the fabric square and iron under a narrow turning to the reverse around the edges. Sew on the ricrac braid all around on the right side, catching in the turned edges. Attach the hearts to one corner of the napkin using double-sided adhesive web, following the instructions on page 66. Finally, decorate using the heart stamp with glitter foil.

Book cover

Notebook, 22.2 x 15.2cm (8¾ x 6in) • Check fabric in turquoise, 25cm (9¾ in) • Cotton fabric in white, 25cm (9¾ in) • Spotted fabric in lime green, 16cm (6¼ in) • Ricrac braid in lime green, 50cm (19¾ in) • Vintage picture: roses • Textile adhesive • Pattern on page 72

Cut out rectangles of the check fabric and the white cotton fabric, 25 × 44cm (9¾ × 17¼in). Place right sides together and sew together at a distance of 1cm (½in) from the edge. Leave 6cm (2¼in) open along one edge for turning out. Trim the seam allowances, turn out, iron the seams flat and close up the opening by hand.

Iron around the narrow sides for a width of 5cm (2in) on the white fabric side and topstitch the upper and lower edges close to the edge. Attach the oval of spotted fabric with double-sided adhesive web according to the instructions on page 66, and glue on the ricrac braid and the picture of the rose.

Butterfly

Spotted fabric in lime green, 12cm (4¾ in) • Cotton fabric in white, 12cm (4¾ in) • Check fabric remnant in turquoise • Iron-on glitter foil in turquoise • Decorative braid in light blue, 40cm (15¾ in) • Flower stamp • Wadding • Double-sided adhesive web, e.g. Vliesofix • Textile adhesive • Pattern on page 72

Reinforce the spotted wings with white fabric using double-sided adhesive web on the reverse (see instructions on page 66) and decorate with the blue pattern and the flower stamp. Sew both pieces together using zigzag stitch – do not close the last 3cm (1¼in) until you have filled the butterfly. Finally, stick on the decorative braid in the centre to act as a hanger.

Who Wants to Play with Me?

Doll

Cotton fabric in skin tone, 30cm (11¾ in) • Dotted fabrics in white/pink and red/white, 20cm (7¾ in) each • Cotton fabric in patterned white/red/pink, 15cm (6in) • Doll's hair in light blonde, 15 x 25cm (6 x 9¾ in) • White button, Ø 1cm (½ in) • Flower buttons in white, 5 x Ø 3mm (⅛ in) and 2 x Ø 6mm (¼ in) • Three wooden flower beads in pink and red, Ø 1cm (½ in) • Three rocaille beads in white • Check ribbon in red/white, 8mm (⅜ in) wide, 2 x 15cm (6in) • Embroidery thread in black and white • Seam sealer • Red colouring pencil • Patterns on pages 73–75

Body

Cut out all the pieces according to the pattern. Paint on seam sealer around the nose piece and leave to dry. Now sew two ear pieces together right sides facing, leaving the straight side open, and turn the ears out. Wrap the corners of the ears towards the centre and secure with a couple of stitches.

Sew the pieces for the arms and legs together right sides facing, leaving an opening for turning out, and then turn the limbs out. Next, stitch together the pieces for the body and head in the same way, incorporating the ears at the marked places. Make sure that the ears point in the right direction! Leave the body open underneath and turn out through the opening.

Fill all the pieces with wadding. Turn the seam allowance for the body inside, push the legs into the body from below and close up the seam.

Close up the arms using mattress stitch and sew them to the body. For this, sew on a strong thread to the underside of an arm. Using a long needle, first pierce through the arm on the outside, then pass the needle through the arm and the body. Pierce through the other arm from the inside to the outside and then again from the outside through the arm and the body. Pass the thread from inside to outside through the first arm and pull tight so that the shoulders are slightly pulled together.

The face is embroidered as in the picture. Sew a gathering stitch around the nose, lightly fill it and sew on to the face using mattress stitch. Attach the hair at the centre of the head using a few stitches, then make two plaits and decorate with the ribbon and flower beads. Draw on the rosy cheeks with the red colouring pencil.

Clothing

Cut out all the pieces according to the pattern. Neaten the top and bottom edges of the pants, turn up and sew in place. Sew together each pair of pieces for the pants, right sides together, along the side seams. Turn one leg out and push it into the other one, so that the centre seams are lying on top of one another. Close them up and turn out the pants. Pull the pants on to the doll and secure with a few stitches.

Close up the shoulder seams of the shirt and sew together the collar pieces right sides together, leaving an opening at the base of the neck. Turn the collar out and sew along the edge at the base of the neck right sides together, following the markings. Now neaten the sleeve seams, turn up and sew. First pass the sleeves right sides together into the armholes and then close up the sleeves and side seams of the shirt.

Neaten the bottom edge of the shirt, turn up and sew. Turn in the right fastening edge in the same way and sew. Pull the shirt on to the doll, place the fastening edges on top of one another and close up the shirt with a few stitches.

For the tunic, lay the pieces for the facing on to the front and back pieces, right sides together, and sew together along the edges around the neckline and armholes. Turn the pieces out and topstitch close to the edge around the neckline. Neaten the bottom edge of the tunic, turn up and sew.

Place the front and back pieces right sides together and close up the side seams. Turn the tunic out and pull it on to the doll. Place the seam allowances at the shoulders on top of one another. Close up the shoulder seams with a few straight stitches and sew the 6mm-diameter (¼in) buttons on to the shoulder seams. Attach the remaining buttons as in the picture.

For the shoes, sew the facing piece to the upper edge of the shoe, right sides together, turn inside and topstitch close to the edge. Place the shoes right sides together along the fold of the fabric and sew the top and bottom seams. Turn the shoes out and decorate with running stitch along the top edge. Pull on the shoes and secure to the feet with a few stitches if necessary.

Attractive Gift Bags

Large bag

Patterned card in blue/white and white/blue, each 30 x 30cm (11¾ x 11¾ in)
• Pieces of coloured card in white (base) and red (heart) • Satin cord in red, 50cm
(19¾ in) • Double-sided adhesive tape, 8mm (⅜ in) wide • Hole punch
• Patterns on page 75 and sheet A

First, cut out the individual pieces, punch the holes and lightly score the lines for the folds on the reverse of the card using a cutter, so that they will fold more easily.

❁

Attach double-sided adhesive tape to the adhesive tabs on the front and then fix all the side pieces to the adhesive tabs on the base one at a time. Fold the side pieces along the horizontal lines and join together.

❁

Fold the side pieces along the short vertical fold lines at the curved edge and thread the satin cord through the holes. Attach both hearts to the ends of the satin cord and carefully draw the cords together, then tie to close the bag.

———⟨ᴑᴑᴑ⟩———

Small bag

Patterned card in red/light blue/white, 30 x 30cm (11¾ x 11¾ in)
• Piece of coloured card in spotted pink/white • Satin cord in red, 35cm
(13¾ in) • Double-sided adhesive tape, 8mm (⅜ in) wide
• Double-sided sticky pad • Hole punch • Patterns on page 75 and sheet A

Cut out the bag and the heart and score all the lines for the folds on the reverse of the card as described above. Fix the double-sided adhesive tape to the front of the tabs and fold in the tabs and the side edges that are folded outwards.

❁

Join the sides of the card and close the base. Now fold the side pieces inwards from the top edge along the fold line and make the fastening. To do this, fold the top flap down and, using the hole punch, punch two holes through all the layers of card approximately 2cm (¾in) from the side edges. Now pull the satin cord through and attach the heart using the double-sided sticky pad and the bag is complete.

From the Heart

Small heart

Patterned cotton fabric remnants in red/white/pink • Check and dotted card in pink/white, A5 • Craft felt in white, 4mm (¼in) thick, A5 • Volume fleece, e.g. H640, 15cm (6in) • Double-sided adhesive web, e.g. Vliesofix, 15cm (6in) • Two red heart buttons, Ø 1cm (½in) • Embroidery thread in white and red • Pattern on page 68

Match up the pairs of fabric with both double-sided adhesive web (see page 66) and volume fleece and join them together by ironing. Cut out the hearts according to the pattern and finish off around the edge with blanket stitch.

Cut out the card hearts and six spacers from felt approximately 1.5cm (⅝in) diameter. Join all the hearts together with a needle and thread as shown, with a spacer between each one. Finally, glue on the buttons and attach some embroidery thread to hang them by.

Gift tag

Pieces of coloured card in dark red, pink/white check and embossed white • Heart button in red, Ø 1cm (½in) • Satin ribbon in dark red, 30cm (11¾in) • Hole punch • Pattern on page 68

First, cut out all the pieces and punch the hole. Now glue the little tags to one another, attach the button and tie on the satin ribbon.

Card

Floral fabric in pink, 15cm (6in) • Coloured card in dotted pink/white, 30 x 20cm (11¾ x 7¾in), and remnants in pink/white check and white • Volume fleece, e.g. H640, 10cm (4in) • Double-sided adhesive web, e.g. Vliesofix, 10cm (4in) • Satin ribbon in dark red, 7mm (⅜in) wide, 70cm (27½in) • Five red heart buttons, Ø 1cm (½in) • Red embroidery thread • Pattern on page 68

As described for the small heart, join the pieces of fabric together with the volume fleece and double-sided adhesive web, then cut out the heart and edge with blanket stitch. Fold the dotted coloured card in two and stick on four white rectangles, 2.5 x 5cm (1 x 2in), and the buttons. Now attach the large square, 10 x 10cm (4 x 4in) and the heart in the centre and glue the satin ribbon strips over the edges of the paper.

Toadstools

Two sheets of plain A4 paper • Red cotton fabric, 25cm (9¾in) • Twenty-four white buttons • Wadding • Hot glue • Pattern sheet A

Cut out the stalks from plain paper and glue them together. Sew together the fabric pieces for the pointed tops of the toadstools along the seam allowance of the straight edge, right sides together, and turn out.

Gather in the tops using a needle and thread, leaving just a small hole underneath, and fill with wadding. Now attach the buttons using hot glue and glue the tops on to the stalks. Hey presto!

To make it easier: you can also glue the pointed toadstool tops together, right sides facing. Allow the adhesive to dry thoroughly before you turn them out.

Garland

Coloured card in red and white/yellow check, A4 • Spotted ribbon in green, 90cm (35½in) • Four white buttons • Watering can, approximately 9cm (3½in) wide • 3D adhesive dots • Pattern on page 77

Cut out the individual flower pieces using the pattern and join together with the 3D adhesive dots. Glue on the buttons to form the centres of the flowers. Tie the watering can in the centre of the ribbon and glue on the individual flowers at equal distances apart. Allow the flowers to dry thoroughly so that the paper adheres properly to the ribbon.

Mini Toadstools

A Cup of Coffee, Please!

Placemat

Floral fabric in red/pink, 50cm (19¾in)
• Check fabric in pink, 50cm (19¾in)
• Fabric remnant in pink with roses
• Ricrac braid in pink, 65cm (25½in)
• Decorative braids in pink/red, 30cm
(11¾in) • Volume fleece, e.g. H640, 50cm
(19¾in) • Double-sided adhesive web, e.g.
Vliesofix • Pattern sheet B

Cut out the large heart from the floral fabric, check fabric and volume fleece. Join the medium-sized and the small heart to the floral heart using double-sided adhesive web, according to the instructions on page 66. Iron the volume fleece on to the reverse. Now sew the large hearts together, right sides facing, following the width of the sewing machine foot and leave a hole for turning out.

❋

Trim the seam allowance, turn out the placemat and close up the opening by hand. Iron the heart out and then sew on the ricrac braid. The small heart is edged with pink braid. All that remains is to add the bow and the placemat is finished.

━━⟨∾⟩━━

Crockery

Tea or coffee set in white porcelain
• Porcelain paint in white, pink and red
• Fine-haired paintbrush • Pattern on page 78

Transfer the cupcake to the desired spot on the teapot using the tracing paper method (see page 66). You can enlarge or reduce the cupcake as you wish beforehand using a photocopier or computer scanner, so that it fits on the piece of crockery you have selected. Paint the cupcake with porcelain paint. Apply the paint thinly so that it doesn't run, and then fix according to the manufacturer's instructions.

Cake stand

Wooden cake stand • Paper napkin in spotted pink and in pink with roses
• Ricrac braid in pink • White acrylic paint • Découpage varnish
• Textile adhesive • Pinking shears

Prime the cake stand with white paint and, when dry, measure the internal diameter of the plate. Cut out a circle of the corresponding size from the spotted napkin using the pinking shears. Attach it to the plate using the découpage varnish as described on page 66.

Cut out a rose motif from the second napkin and attach this to the plate using the découpage varnish. Now cover the whole cake stand with découpage varnish to seal it and, when dry, glue on the ricrac braid.

Card

Patterned paper in light blue/pink, 27 x 13.5cm (10¾ x 5¼ in) • Pink paper, 13.5 x 4cm (5¼ x 1½ in)
• Paper napkin with cups and in pink with roses • Decorative braid in pink/red, 25.5cm (10in)
• Rose button in pink • Découpage varnish

Either add the wording to the pink-coloured paper before cutting it out, using your computer and printer, or add it afterwards by hand. Fold the patterned paper in two to make a card and glue the pink paper flush to the top of the card.

Place the decorative braid on the card and make a simple bow, finished width 6cm (2¼in), using the diagram on page 75, and attach it to the card with the button. Cut out a cup and various roses from the napkins and fix them to the patterned paper following the instructions on page 66. Only varnish the lower part where the motifs are, otherwise the paper will stain and buckle.

Place card

Scrap of patterned paper in light blue/pink • Decorative braid in light blue/pink/red, 20cm (7¾in)
• Red felt-tip pen • Pattern on page 70

Cut out the spoon according to the pattern, tie the decorative braid around in a bow and write the name on the handle in felt-tip pen. Hey presto!

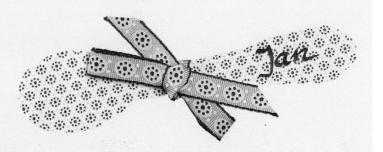

Tea cosy

Cotton fabric in white, 30cm (11¾in) • Cotton fabric in light blue/pink, 15cm (6in) • Cotton fabric in red/white, 15cm (6in) • Floral fabric in pink/red, 15cm (6in) • Check fabric in pink, 15cm (6in) • Ricrac braid in pink, 70cm (27½in) • Decorative braid in red/pink and light blue/pink, 70cm (27½in) • Decorative braid in pink/red, 30cm (11¾in) • Heart button in pink • Double-sided adhesive volume fleece, e.g. HH650, 30cm (11¾in) • Textile adhesive • Pattern sheet A

Cut out the basic shape twice, from white cotton fabric and volume fleece. The pattern pieces A, B and C are each cut twice from the patterned fabrics. For the roses, you will also need two 10 × 15cm (4 × 6in) pieces of fabric. The loop is made from a strip 12 × 3cm (4¾ × 1¼in).

Start with the loop: iron together the long edges of the strip of fabric, iron them back over to the folded edge, then topstitch the open long edge close to the edge.

Now place the white fabric pieces beneath the volume fleece and place the patterned pieces A, B and C on to the fleece so they are flush with each other. Secure everything firmly using the iron, then cut up the decorative braids and stitch them over the cut edges. Neaten the bottom edge with zigzag stitch.

Sew the front and back pieces together with a narrow zigzag stitch, wrong sides together, catching in the loop for the hanger at the same time. The bottom edge stays open and is glued with ricrac braid. Make the roses as described on page 67 and sew them on by hand, together with the bow and the button.

Cupcake garland

Various patterned papers in red/pink/light blue,
30 x 30cm (11¾ x 11¾in)
• Ricrac braid in white and pink, 50cm (19¾in)
• Pink satin ribbon, at least 2m (78¾in)
• Paper flowers in turquoise, Ø 1.5cm (⅝in)
and 2.5cm (1in) • Double-sided adhesive tape
• Textile adhesive • Pattern on page 70

For each cupcake, cut out both pattern
pieces twice and join each together with
adhesive tape. Glue both pieces with the
ricrac braid and decorate with paper
flowers, cut-out roses or other
paper patterns.

Join together the front and back sides of
the cupcakes with the satin ribbon in
between, 12cm (4¾in) apart, so that the
satin ribbon sits slightly above the centre
of each cake. If you wish, you can also
attach individual paper flowers between
the cupcakes.

Home Sweet Home

We like our homes to be inviting and a space where we can unwind and be ourselves. The bathroom, bedroom and the study are places of refuge, where we can enjoy peace and quiet and time to let our thoughts wander; they are places to escape to, where we can be creative or simply get lost in a good book. The cosier we make this sanctuary, the more refreshing it is to spend time there. So just relax and enjoy the peace and quiet!

Sweet Dreams

Fleece cushion

Wool felt in pink, 50cm (19¾in) • Cotton fabric remnants in dotted brown and brown with roses • Dotted ribbon in pink, 30cm (11¾in) • Ricrac braid in brown, 65cm (25½in) • Pompom braid in pink, 1.5m (59in) • Wadding • Double-sided adhesive web, e.g. Vliesofix • Textile adhesive • Pattern sheet B

Cut out the large heart twice from wool felt, then attach the small and medium-sized hearts with double-sided adhesive web following the instructions on page 66. Edge the medium-sized heart with ricrac braid.

Now stitch the wool hearts together right sides facing, catching in the pompom braid at the same time. Make sure that all the pompoms are pointing inwards and leave 15cm (6in) open for turning. Turn the heart out, press open the seam and fill the cushion with wadding. Sew up the opening by hand and decorate the cushion with a pink bow.

Heart garland

Styropor heart, 15cm (6in) high • Cotton fabric in dotted brown, 20cm (7¾in) • Wool felt remnants in pink • Compressed volume fleece, e.g. Thermolam 272, 20cm (7¾in) • Decorative braid in brown/pink, 60cm (23½in) • Satin ribbon in pink and brown, 5mm (¼in) wide, 1.2m (47¼in) • Pins without heads • Twelve little decorative pink roses • Flower stem wire • Textile adhesive

Make a long strip from compressed volume fleece, 6cm × 2.2m (2¼ × 86½in), and from dotted fabric, 7cm × 2.2m (2¾ × 86½in). First, cover the heart with the fleece, then wrap the fabric around, having first ironed over one long edge of the fabric strip by 1cm (½in) so that the raw edge is hidden. Secure the start and finish with textile adhesive or turn up and secure with a few stitches.

For the roses, cut the wool felt into pieces 2 × 5cm (¾ × 2in), cutting the ends off at an angle. Roll the felt strips into rose shapes and wind them together underneath with the flower stem wire. Tie on satin bows and pin the flowers to the garland. Tie on the decorative braid as a hook and the garland is ready!

Lampshade

Pink lampshade, e.g. Ø 16cm (6½in), 28cm (11in) high
- Dotted ribbon in pink, 50cm (19¾in)
- Ricrac braid in brown, 50cm (19¾in)
- Pompom braid in pink, 50cm (19¾in)
- Textile adhesive

Measure the circumference of the shade at the place where the braid will be attached – here, it is 7cm (2¾in) above the bottom edge. Cut the braids accordingly, allowing an extra 1.5cm (⅝in) for the dotted braid. Glue the ricrac braid behind the pompom braid, so that the wavy edge sticks out just above it and attach both to the shade. Attach the dotted braid on top, turn in the end and glue in place.

Box

Cardboard box with lid, 12 x 12cm (4¾ x 4¾in)
- Wool felt remnant in pink • Three pink pompoms
- Small decorative rose • Decorative braid in brown, 75cm (29½in) • Ricrac braid in brown, 60cm (23½in)
- Gift wrap in dotted pink • Double-sided adhesive tape
- Double-sided adhesive web, e.g. Vliesofix
- Textile adhesive

Cover the box and lid with double-sided adhesive web and adhesive tape respectively, following the instructions on page 66, and then cover with wool felt and gift wrap. Glue on the ricrac braid and the decorative braid. To decorate the lid, glue the pompoms to each other and edge the lid with ricrac braid. Finally, add the rose and the bow.

Bookmark

Felt remnant in pink • Cotton fabric remnants in dotted brown and in brown with roses • Ricrac braid in pink, 50cm (19¾in) • Decorative braid in brown, 50cm (19¾in) • Double-sided adhesive web, e.g. Vliesofix • Textile adhesive • Pattern on page 78

As described on page 11 (bag pendant), make a felt heart and cover both sides with fabric, incorporating the decorative braid folded in two and glued together, so that you can place the braid inside your book. Using double-sided adhesive web, attach a fabric rose on to the dotted side of the heart as described on page 66. Finally, glue ricrac braid on to both sides of the heart.

Coat hanger

Adult coat hanger and children's coat hanger in wood • Cotton fabric in dotted brown and brown with roses, 20cm (7¾in) • Wool felt remnant in pink • Volume fleece, e.g. H630, 20cm (7¾in) • Decorative braid in dotted brown, 1m (39½in), and dotted pink, 80cm (31½in) • Pompom braid in pink, 1m (39½in) • Double-sided adhesive web, e.g. Vliesofix • Textile adhesive • Patterns on page 78 and sheet B

Cut out the pattern piece twice from fabric and twice from fleece, then iron the fleece on to the reverse of the fabric pieces. Secure the felt heart together, with the fabric rose attached to one of the pieces, using double-sided adhesive web (see instructions on page 66).

Sew the fabric pieces together 1cm (½in) from the edge, right sides together, leaving the bottom long edge open. Turn the fabric out. Insert the hanger without the hook and then carefully push the hook through the seam and screw into the hanger.

Neaten the raw edges together with zigzag stitch. Sew the pompom braid to the front along the edge and cover the seam on both sides with the decorative braid.

Lovable Little Lamb

Little lamb

Fleece fabric remnant in white • Check fabric remnant in green
• Piece of photo card in white • Piece of coloured card in grey
• Two wobbly eyes, Ø 3mm (⅛in) • Twenty flower buttons in
white, dark pink or light pink • Paper wire in white and dark red,
30cm (11¾in) each • Three round wooden sticks in green,
approximately 20cm (7¾in) • Double-sided adhesive tape
• Hot glue • Pattern on page 76

First, glue the fabric to the photo card to strengthen it
using the adhesive tape and then cut out all the motifs.
Paint on the sheep's face and attach the wobbly eyes.
Attach the flower buttons to the bushes and the sheep's
coat using adhesive. Wrap the paper wire around a
wooden stick to make a spiral.

Glue the three pieces of the sheep together. Using hot
glue, attach the sticks to the reverse of the sheep and
the bushes. Wind the wire spirals around the sheep's
stick and, if necessary, secure with hot glue.

*To make it easier: if you cannot find any round, green wooden
sticks, then just use three kebab sticks and paint them
with green acrylic paint.*

A Special Place
to Make Time
for Myself

Lampshade

White lampshade • Paper napkin in pink with roses • Découpage varnish • Pre-folded bias binding in dotted pink • Textile adhesive

Cut out the various roses from the napkin and attach them to the lampshade using the découpage varnish, according to the instructions on page 66. Leave the varnish to dry and then cover the entire shade with découpage varnish.

Now take the bias binding and iron it in half. Once the varnish is dry, you can edge the top and bottom with the binding (by gluing). Fold the end in by 1cm (½in).

Desk pad

Grey cardboard, 3mm (⅛in) thick, 60 x 50cm (23½ x 19¾in) • Paper napkins in pink with roses and in spotted green • Ricrac braid in pink, 2.3m (90½in) • Decorative braid in red/white stripes, 2.3m (90½in) • Découpage varnish • White acrylic paint • Textile adhesive

Paint the card on one side with white acrylic paint and, when dry, attach the whole spotted napkin to the centre using découpage varnish (see instructions on page 66). Now attach a rose to the centre and make a border to the pad with individual pieces torn out of the napkin. When dry, glue ricrac braid and decorative braid to the outer edge.

Boxes and tins

Box or tin • Paper napkins in spotted pink or green, or with roses • Decorative braid, e.g. in red/white stripes, 1cm (½in) wide, or with rose pattern, 4cm (1½in) wide • Ricrac braid in pink • Heart-shaped buttons, if desired • White acrylic paint • Clear varnish • Découpage varnish • Textile adhesive

If needed, first paint the box or tin in white all over and leave to dry. If you don't want to attach any napkin motifs, then cover the paint with a coat of clear varnish.

Otherwise, attach the desired motifs using découpage varnish (instructions on page 66) and then cover everything with a layer of découpage varnish for protection. When dry, decorate the box or tin with ribbons, ricrac braid or buttons. A diagram for the bow on the round tin can be found on page 75.

Pincushion

Cotton fabric in white with little roses, 20cm (7¾in) • Ricrac braid in pink, 60cm (23½in) • Decorative braid in red/white stripes, 30cm (11¾in) • Heart button in pink • Wadding • Textile adhesive • Pattern sheet B

Cut out the heart twice from fabric with a 1cm (½in) seam allowance. Sew the pieces together, right sides facing, and leave an opening for turning. Trim the seam allowance and turn out.

Iron out the seam and fill the heart with wadding, then close the opening by hand. Finally, glue the ricrac braid around the outside edge and decorate the heart with a bow and the button.

My Old
Jeddy Bear

Teddy

Mohair fabric in dark brown with light brown hair, 8mm (⅜in) long, 25cm (9¾in)
• Button in olive, Ø 6mm (¼in) • Black embroidery thread • Wadding • Granules
• Red colouring pencil • Patterns on pages 76 and 77

Cut out all the pieces according to the pattern. Sew each of the two pieces for the arms, legs and ears together, right sides facing, and turn out through the openings. Fill the feet and hands with some granules and then fill the rest of the arms and legs with wadding. Sew up the legs at the open edges inside the seam allowance and close up the openings for turning on the arms using mattress stitch.

Now sew the head and body pieces right sides together as far as the opening for turning. Turn the body out and fill with wadding. Turn the seam allowance towards the inside at the opening for turning. Push the legs into the body from below and close up the opening.

Sew on the teddy's ears using mattress stitch. Attach the arms as for the doll on page 29. Trim the hair on the face and on the inside of the ears and hands using scissors. Embroider the face and sew on the button for the eye. Finally, redden the cheeks with the colouring pencil.

Wooden basket

Wooden basket • Various patterned cards in white, pink, red and light blue,
30 x 30cm (11¾ x 11¾in) • Fine-grade sandpaper • Bookbinder's glue • Paintbrush

Cut out eight rectangles to decorate each long side of the wooden basket, making sure that the edges that are stuck next to one another match exactly. Leave an excess of 1cm (½in) for the outer sides. This will be trimmed once the pieces have been glued in place to make sure that they fit the outside edges of the wooden basket. Also cut the paper pieces for the short sides of the box leaving a 1cm (½in) excess.

Now attach the rectangles to the long sides working from the middle outwards towards the edge using bookbinder's glue. Make sure that the edges lie flush with one another and press down well. When dry, cut off the excess paper along the edges of the box. Now proceed with the sides in the same way. Finally, carefully sand all the sides with sandpaper.

To make it easier: bookbinder's glue dries relatively quickly, which is why you should spread the glue gradually over the larger areas and only use as much as would be needed to attach one or two paper rectangles.

Somewhere to Relax

Candleholder

Wooden candleholder • White acrylic paint • Clear varnish • Check fabric in pink, 10 x 10cm (4 x 4in) • Various decorative patterned braids in light blue, red and pink • Ricrac braid in white • Textile adhesive

Paint the candleholder with the white paint and, when dry, seal it with clear varnish. Glue the various decorative braids and the ricrac braid to the candleholder. Make a fabric rosette from the check fabric following the instructions on page 67. Sew the fabric rosette to a piece of decorative braid and tie to the candleholder.

Tissue box cover

Wooden decorative cover • Check fabric in pink, 10 x 10cm (4 x 4in) • Paper napkin in spotted turquoise • Pompom braid in light blue, 70cm (27½in) • Decorative braid in dotted blue and dotted pink, 70cm (27½in) and 30cm (11¾in) respectively • White acrylic paint • Découpage varnish • Textile adhesive

First, make a fabric rosette following the instructions on page 67 and paint the cover with white paint. When dry, glue the spotted napkin to the top (see instructions on page 66) and apply découpage varnish to the whole cover. Decorate the finished cover with the fabric rosette, the pompom braid and the decorative braid.

Door plaque

Door plaque, oval, 17.5 x 7.5cm (7 x 3in) • Cotton fabric remnants in light blue and light blue floral • Paper napkin in light blue check • Ricrac braid in white, 50cm (19¾in) • Decorative patterned braid in light blue/pink, 30cm (11¾in) • Lacquered wire in red, 40cm (15¾in) • White modelling clay • White acrylic paint • Découpage varnish • Double-sided adhesive web, e.g. Vliesofix • Textile adhesive • Pinking shears

By following the instructions on page 67, make a fabric rosette of diameter 4.5cm (1¾in) and decorate with a bow. Paint the door plaque white and cover with the check napkin (see instructions on page 66).

Glue the ricrac braid on to the reverse of the plaque so that it juts out a little all around the edge. Cut the edge using pinking shears then attach a 12 x 5cm (4¾ x 2in) strip of fabric to the plaque using double-sided adhesive web, following the instructions on page 66.

Next, make the letters from modelling clay and leave to dry according to the manufacturer's instructions and then glue to the centre of the plaque. All that remains is the fabric rosette and the wire for hanging and then your plaque is ready.

Tins

Round tins • Towelling remnants in turquoise • Floral fabric remnants in turquoise • Spotted fabric remnant in light blue • Paper napkin in light blue check • Different decorative braids in light blue, pink and red • Pompom braid in light blue • Woven interfacing, e.g. G700 • White acrylic paint • Découpage varnish • Clear varnish • Textile adhesive

First paint the edge of the lid and the top edge of the tin only (if the lower part is going to be covered with fabric), corresponding to the width of the lid, and then protect the paint with clear varnish.

Next, either attach a design from the napkin using the découpage varnish (instructions on page 66) or glue fabric on to the tin using the woven interfacing. Do not cover the painted edge of the tin, otherwise the lid will not fit later. Cover the lid with towelling fabric using the woven interfacing and then decorate the lids and the tins with fabric rosettes (instructions on page 67), pompoms, braids and bows.

Fish

Towelling in turquoise, 15cm (6in) • Fabric remnants in spotted and floral light blue, and pink check • Decorative braid in dotted light blue and floral light blue/red • Pompom braid in light blue • Wadding • Double-sided adhesive web, e.g. Vliesofix • Pattern on page 79

Cut the large pieces twice each from towelling and attach the small fabric pieces to them using double-sided adhesive web, following the instructions on page 66. Sew the pompom braid over the raw edge.

Now sew the fish pieces right sides together, following the width of the sewing machine foot, catching in the ends of a double piece of decorative braid for the loop into the top of the fish body. Leave 6cm (2¼in) open for filling.

Turn the fish out and press open the seams. Now fill the fish with wadding and sew up the opening by hand. Finally, decorate the fish with a pompom for an eye, a fabric rosette (instructions on page 67) and a bow.

Hot water bottle cover

Towelling in turquoise, 30cm (11¾in)
• Floral fabric in light blue, 15cm (6in)
• Check fabric remnant in pink
• Decorative braids in patterned red,
white, light blue and pink
• Ricrac braid in white • Elastic band,
25cm (9¾in) • Pattern sheet B

Cut the hot water bottle piece twice
from towelling and the trim twice
from fabric. Iron over 1cm (½in) of
the trim to the reverse along the
straight edge and sew it close to the
ironed edge on to the towelling
piece. Next sew the ricrac braid,
then the decorative braid
on top, slightly offset.

Now sew the two pieces right sides
together, leaving the opening free.
This is then turned over twice by 1cm
(½in) to the reverse of the fabric and
sewn close to the edge. Sew the
elastic band to the reverse at the
narrowest point under tension and
neaten well. Turn out the cover and
sew on a fabric rosette as a decoration
(instructions on page 67) and adorn
with a bow.

Hand towel

Towelling in turquoise, 91 x 47cm (35¾ x 18½ in) • Floral fabric in light blue, 20 x 47cm (7¾ x 18½ in)
• Check fabric remnant in pink • Decorative braid in red/white stripes, 60cm (23½ in)
• Decorative braid in patterned red/white, 20cm (7¾ in)
• Ricrac braid in white, 50cm (19¾ in)

Make the fabric rosette from the check fabric, Ø 4–5cm (1½–2in) following the instructions on page 67
and decorate with a bow. Cut out the towelling fabric and the fabric for the towel trim, ensuring
that one of the short edges of the towelling fabric is a selvedge edge.

Iron under the floral fabric along one long edge by 1cm (½in) to the reverse of the fabric. Place the opposite side right
sides together on to the short raw edge of the towelling fabric and sew them together 1cm (½in) from the edge. Iron out
the seam and place the trim on to the towelling fabric, so that the seam is covered and the right side of the fabric is
uppermost. Now sew the ironed-under edge of fabric close to the edge.

Sew on the ricrac braid and then the decorative braid on top of the sewing line and slightly offset. The long edges
are then turned up twice by 1cm (½in) and sewn close to the edge. For the loop, cut a 9cm (3½in) piece
of decorative braid, turning in the ends by 1cm (½in) each and attach to the centre
of the selvedge edge on the right side. Finally, sew on the fabric rosette.

The Little Imp Says Goodnight

Box with imp

Card box, oval, 16cm (6¼in) long • Floral fabric in white, 50 x 5cm (19¾ x 2in)
• Fabric remnants in light blue/white stripes, in blue stripes and in white • Piece of coloured
card in skin tone • Woven interfacing, e.g. H 180 • Four red heart buttons, Ø 1cm (½in)
• Metal bell in red, Ø 6mm (¼in) • Parcel string, 4 x 3cm (1½ x 1¼in) long
• Double-sided adhesive tape, 50 x 5cm (19¾ x 2in), plus a scrap
• Acrylic paint in white and yellow • Red sewing thread • Hot glue
• Paintbrush • Pattern on page 78

First, prepare the box by mixing some yellow acrylic paint with white and using it to paint the lid. While the paint is drying, attach double-sided adhesive tape to the reverse of the floral fabric, as well as to the blue striped fabric and to a little piece of the white fabric remnant (pocket). Reinforce the remaining white fabric on the reverse with woven interfacing.

✿

Now cut all the pieces for the imp from coloured card and fabric and make an additional strip 4cm (1½in) wide and 46cm (18in) long from the floral fabric. Sew the pieces for the hat together right sides facing, trim the seam allowance close to the stitching and turn the hat out. Sew on the tiny bell at the tip.

✿

Glue the pocket to the shirt, decorate with a few red stitches and stick the shirt to the box. Edge the neckerchief with ornate stitches too and knot the pointed ends. Secure it over the shirt using hot glue. Draw on the face and attach the parcel string as hair.

✿

Turn the hat under by approximately 1cm (½in) and secure the face into the hat. Glue the head and hat to the lid and add the heart buttons. Finally, glue the floral fabric on to the box itself and hey presto!

Tip: you can adjust the measurements to any size: just alter to fit the size of the box. Make sure that the strip of fabric ends below the lid, otherwise the box won't shut. You can also enlarge or reduce the size of the imp using a photocopier or computer scanner.

General instructions

Your basic equipment

As well as the items given in each list of materials, you should also have some tools and equipment to hand that are always useful. These include:

• Pencil and ruler • Adhesive • Scissors or cutter with cutting base • Sewing machine and sewing thread
• Pins and sewing needles • Tracing paper, dressmaker's tracing paper or thin card (to transfer patterns)

Transferring patterns

Depending on the material and model, there are various methods for transferring patterns.

For paper or uneven surfaces, we recommend the tracing paper method: simply trace the pattern on to tracing paper, cross-hatch over the lines on the reverse using a soft pencil, then place the paper on the desired material and draw over the lines with a hard pencil.

If you need several pattern pieces that are the same, it is worth making up templates by tracing the motif on to tracing paper, roughly cutting it out and gluing it to thin card. Cut out the motif, place the template on the desired material and draw round with a pencil.

It is best to transfer large pattern pieces to the fabric using dressmaker's tracing paper. Trace the pattern piece from the pattern sheet, cut it out, attach it to the fabric with pins, draw on the seam allowance if necessary and cut out.

Tip: the template method is also suitable for cutting smaller pattern pieces.

Découpage technique

For the découpage technique, a paper-napkin motif is glued to a base. You can choose between two methods: the tearing technique and the cutting technique.

Separate the upper, printed layer of the napkin and tear or cut out the desired motif or pattern. Varnish the base with découpage varnish, place the motif on to the pre-varnished area and paint it with découpage varnish so that it binds with the base.

To make it easier: motifs can easily be removed from the napkin by going around the outline with a wet paintbrush.

Working with adhesive web

Double-sided adhesive web, e.g. Vliesofix, is used for applying fabric pieces or motifs. As an alternative, you can also use iron-on stabiliser. Both materials are used in the same way.

Iron the double-sided adhesive web on to the reverse of the desired fabric with the paper side facing upwards. Transfer the pattern on to the paper backing, making sure that you draw the mirror image of the pattern piece.

Now cut out the piece cleanly along the lines. Pull off the paper, place the piece in the desired position and fix with the iron. To protect your iron, place a thin cotton towel in between.

Tip: if you want to attach fabric or paper pieces with double-sided adhesive tape, proceed in the same way as above, omitting ironing.

Working with fabric

Fabric roses

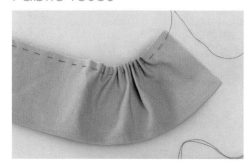

Fold the strips of fabric in half lengthways and sew the open long edges together with a simple running stitch. Draw the fabric together by pulling on the thread, so that it gathers, and roll it up into a rose. Turn in the ends at a 45° angle and secure the rose with a few stitches.

Fabric rosettes

For the fabric rosettes, you need a circle of fabric appropriate for the desired size. Iron around the outside edge turning it in by about 5mm (¼in). Sew around the circle with running stitch as described for the fabric roses and gather. Press the gathered fabric flat. For a fabric rosette with a Ø 4cm (1½in), you will need a circle of fabric with a Ø 8.5cm (3¼in); for a rosette with a Ø 5cm (2in), you will need a circle of fabric with a Ø 10.5cm (4¼in).

Tip: unless stated otherwise, a seam allowance of 1cm (½in) is added to the fabric pieces.

Sewing fabric

To make the models in this book, just a few special stitches are required, such as mattress stitch and blanket stitch.

Mattress stitch

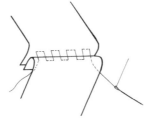

Used for sewing pieces of fabric together. Simply place the pieces on top of one another and pass the thread to and fro between the pieces of fabric, at equal distances apart.

Blanket stitch

Used for neatening and decorating the edges of fabric. Pierce the needle through the fabric about 5mm (¼in) away from the edge and then thread the needle through the resulting loop.

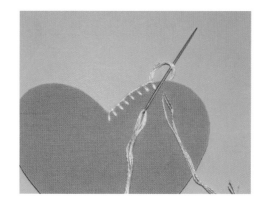

To make it easier:

Fabrics that may be washed later should definitely be washed before they are cut. Otherwise, they may shrink at different rates, making the finished item look lumpy and unattractive.

'Right sides together' means that the pieces of fabric are placed on top of one another with the correct, top sides facing and are then sewn together. 'Wrong sides together' means that the pieces of fabric are placed on top of one another with the incorrect or reverse sides facing.

Tip: the term 'remnant' in the list of materials always refers to a piece that is at most A5, or 15 x 20cm (6 x 7¾in).

If you paint the edges of small pieces of fabric, such as noses or ears, with seam sealer after cutting out, the cut edges will not fray. Leave to dry thoroughly before continuing to work.

It is best to pin two pieces that you want to sew together beforehand, to prevent them from slipping. The more curved the edges, the closer the pins need to be.

Before turning out pieces that have been sewn together, the seam allowance should be trimmed to around 5mm (¼in). At the corners or for circles, the trimmed seam allowance should then also be snipped just as far as the stitching. This prevents the corners or circles from puckering after being turned out.

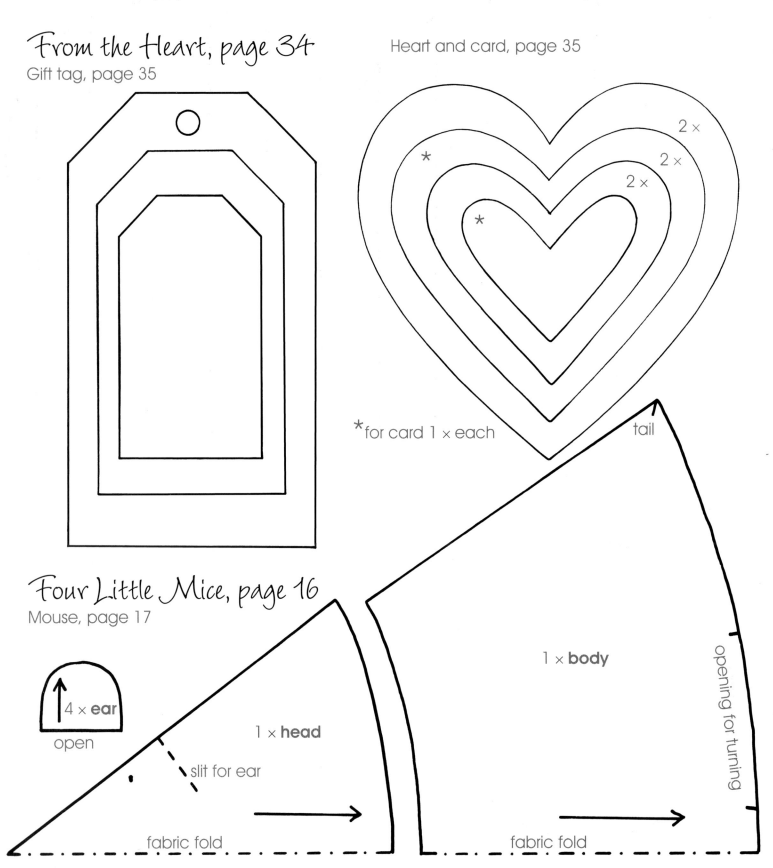

From the Heart, page 34
Gift tag, page 35

Heart and card, page 35

2 ×

2 ×

2 ×

*

*

*for card 1 × each

tail

Four Little Mice, page 16
Mouse, page 17

4 × **ear**

open

slit for ear

1 × **head**

1 × **body**

opening for turning

fabric fold

fabric fold

Four Little Mice,
page 16
Mouse, page 17

Everything in Its
Place, page 8
Clothes hooks, page 12

1 × **base**

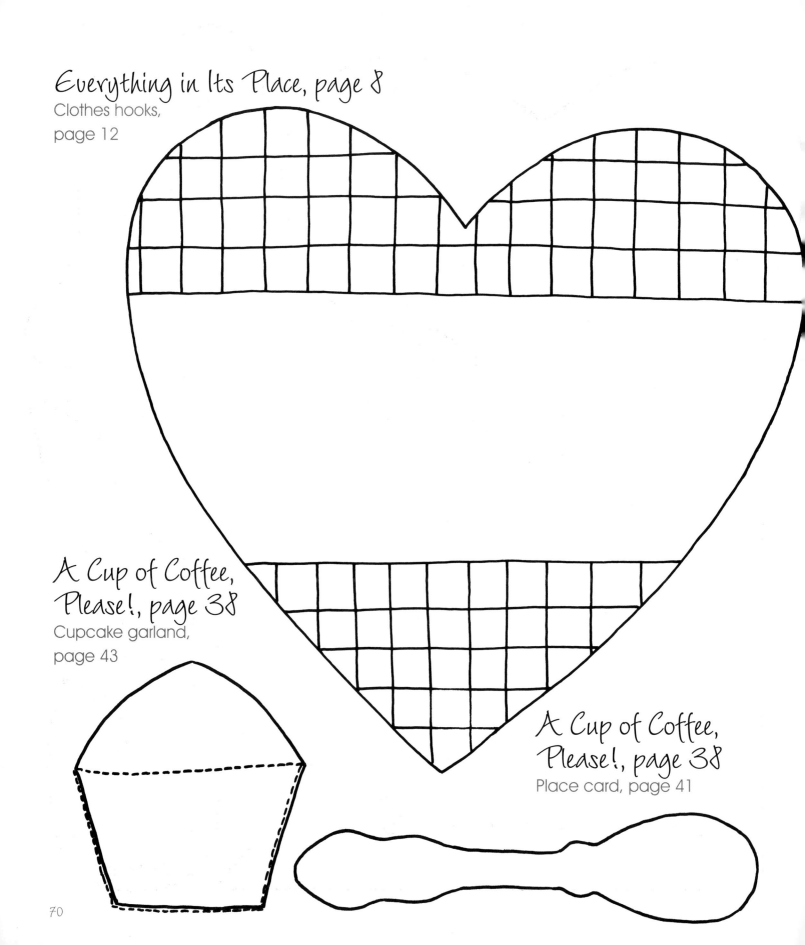

Everything in Its Place, page 8

Clothes hooks,
page 12

A Cup of Coffee,
Please!, page 38

Cupcake garland,
page 43

A Cup of Coffee,
Please!, page 38

Place card, page 41

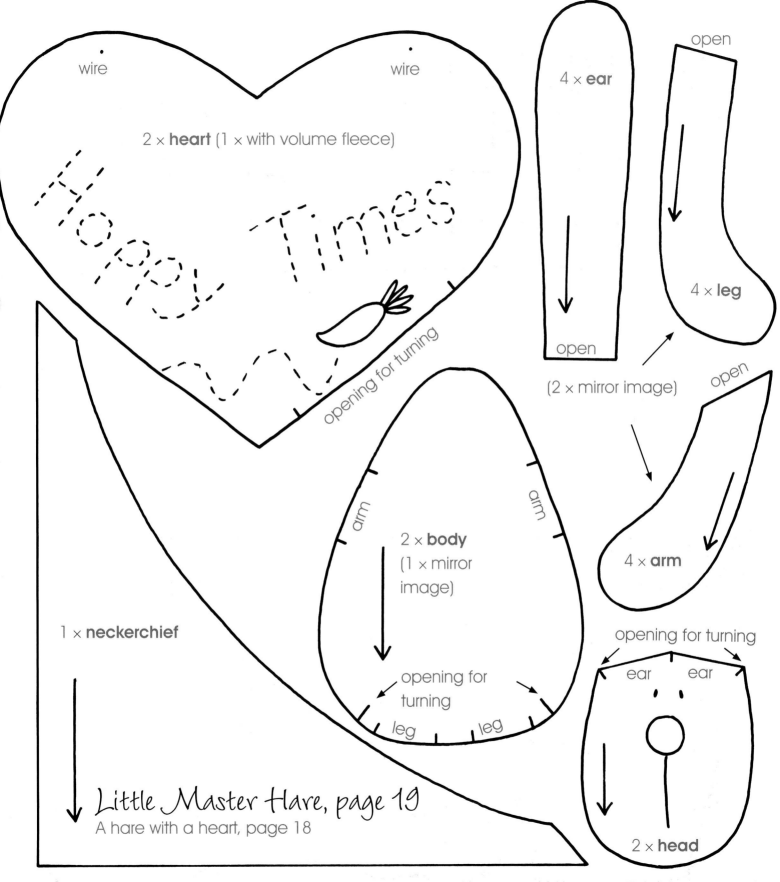

wire

wire

2 × **heart** (1 × with volume fleece)

Happy Times

opening for turning

4 × **ear**

open

open

4 × **leg**

(2 × mirror image)

open

4 × **arm**

1 × **neckerchief**

arm

arm

2 × **body**
(1 × mirror image)

opening for turning

leg

leg

opening for turning

ear

ear

Little Master Hare, page 19
A hare with a heart, page 18

2 × **head**

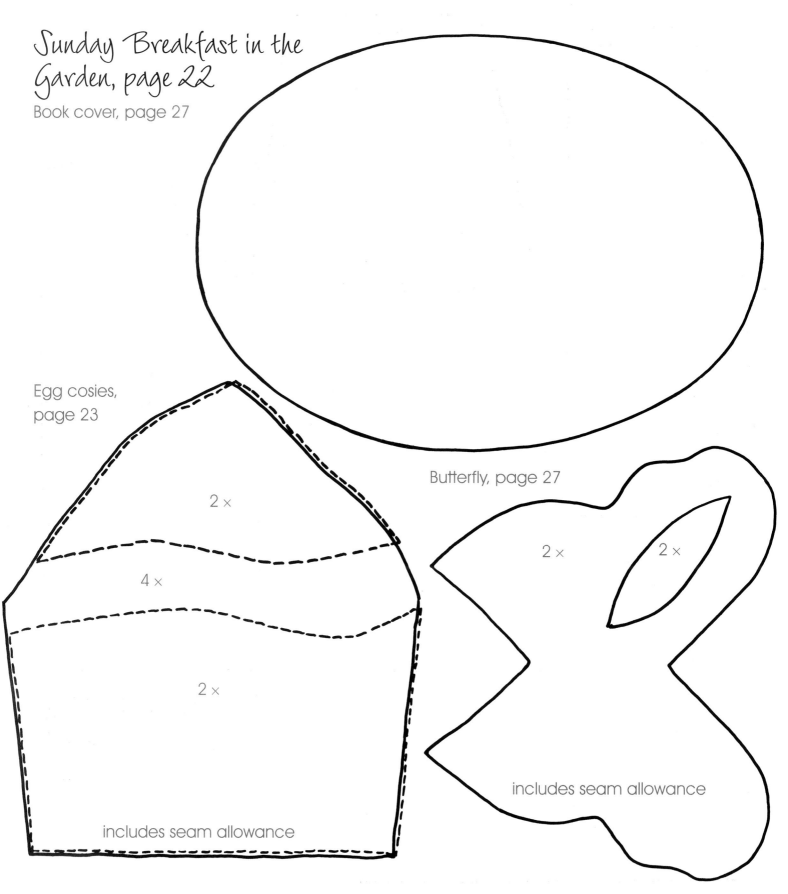

Sunday Breakfast in the Garden, page 22

Book cover, page 27

Egg cosies, page 23

2 ×

4 ×

2 ×

includes seam allowance

Butterfly, page 27

2 ×

2 ×

includes seam allowance

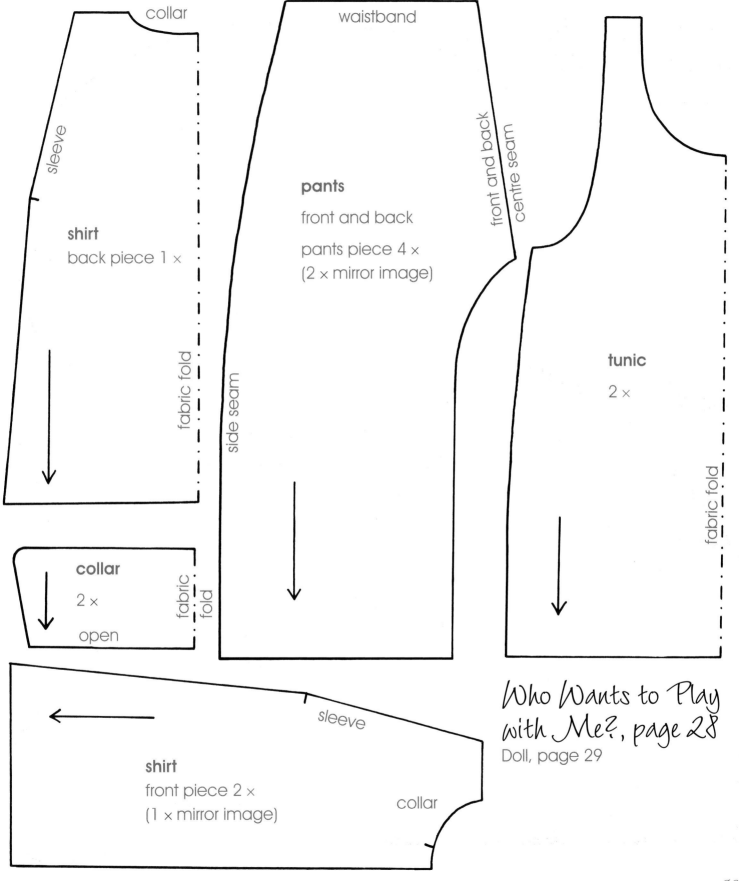

collar

sleeve

shirt
back piece 1 ×

fabric fold

waistband

pants

front and back

pants piece 4 ×
(2 × mirror image)

side seam

front and back centre seam

tunic

2 ×

fabric fold

collar

2 ×

open

fabric fold

shirt
front piece 2 ×
(1 × mirror image)

sleeve

collar

*Who Wants to Play
with Me?, page 28*
Doll, page 29

73

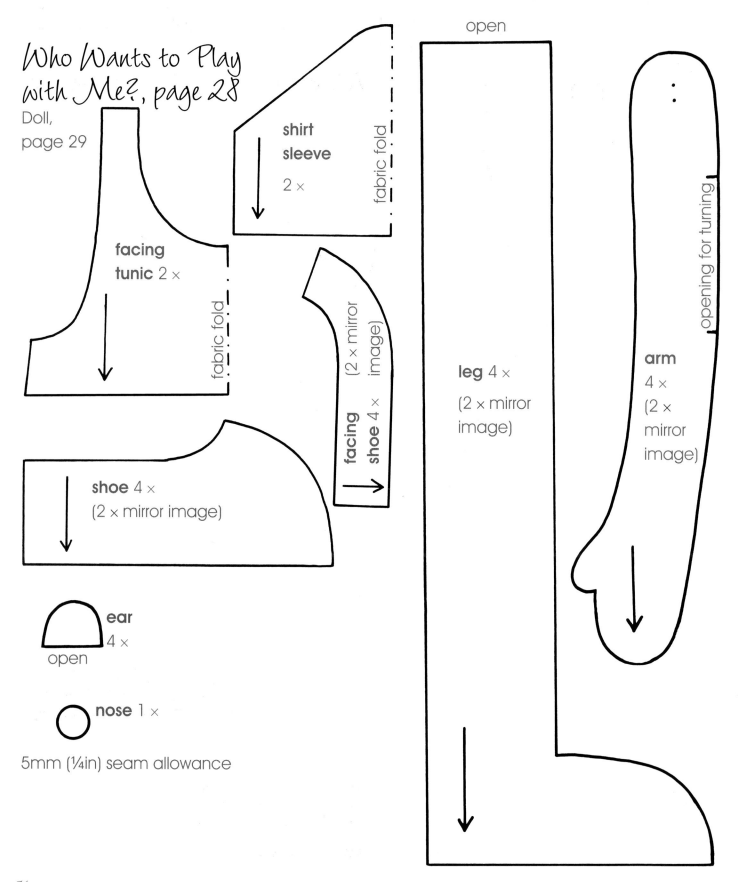

Who Wants to Play with Me?, page 28

Doll, page 29

shirt sleeve 2 ×

fabric fold

facing tunic 2 ×

fabric fold

open

leg 4 × (2 × mirror image)

opening for turning

arm 4 × (2 × mirror image)

facing shoe 4 × (2 × mirror image)

shoe 4 × (2 × mirror image)

ear 4 ×

open

nose 1 ×

5mm (¼in) seam allowance

nose

ear   ear

arm   arm

body/head
piece
2 ×

leg   leg

open

Bows

2

seam

stitch double bow

14cm
(5½in)

8cm
(3¼in)

arrange double bow

arrange single bow

Lovable Little Lamb, page 50

Little lamb, page 51

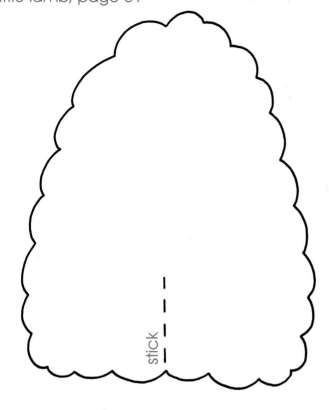

stick

stick

My Old Teddy Bear, page 56

Teddy, page 57

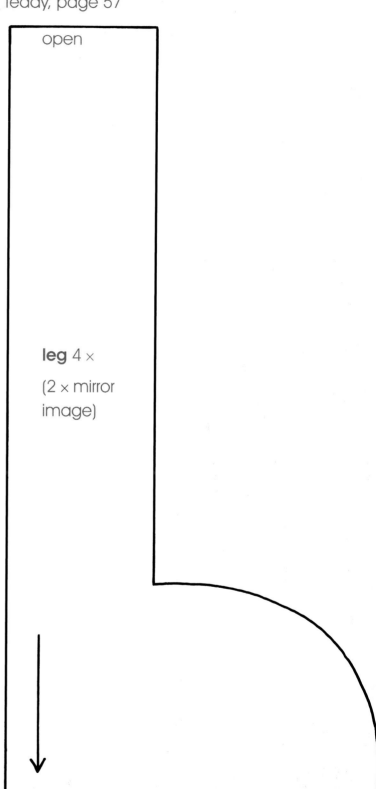

open

leg 4 ×

(2 × mirror image)

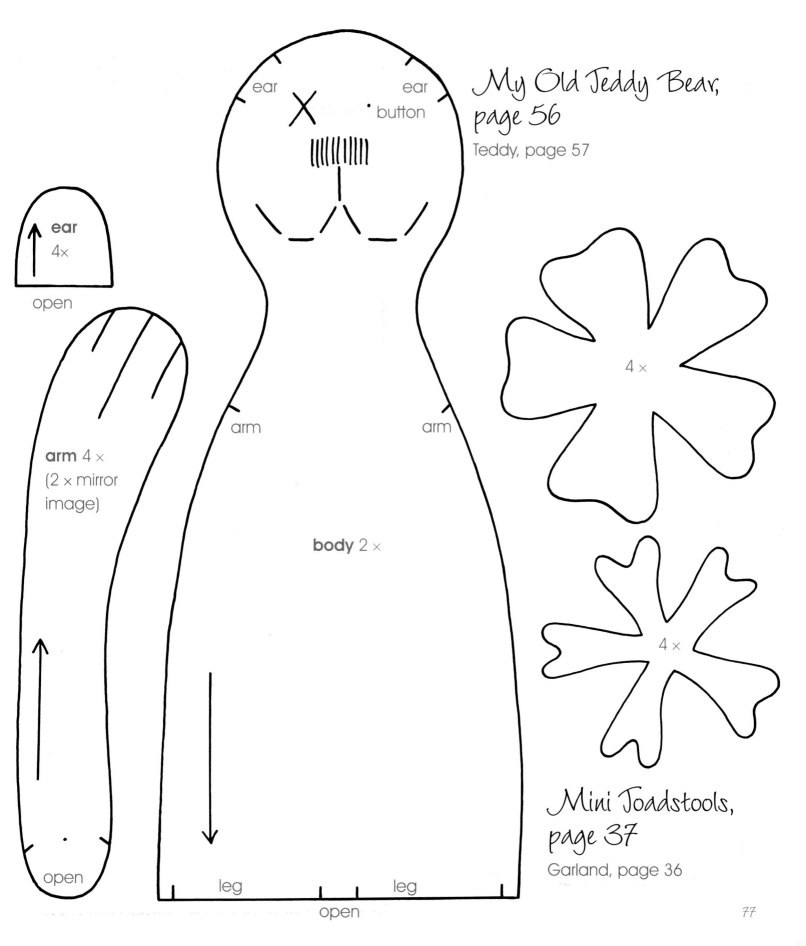

ear

ear · button

My Old Teddy Bear,
page 56

Teddy, page 57

ear
4×

open

arm 4 ×
(2 × mirror
image)

arm

arm

4 ×

body 2 ×

4 ×

open

Mini Toadstools,
page 37

Garland, page 36

leg

leg

open

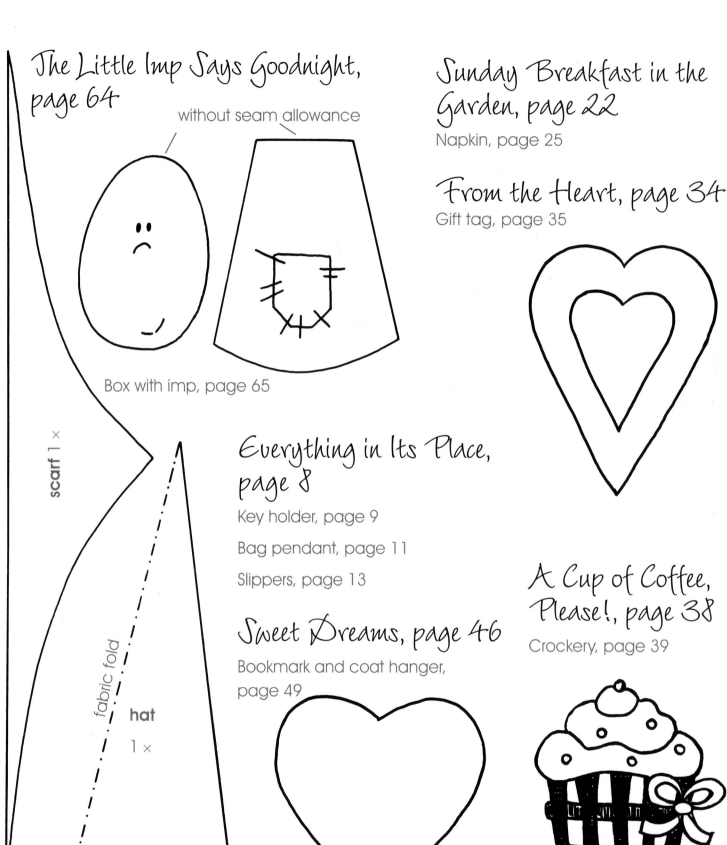

The Little Imp Says Goodnight, page 64

without seam allowance

Box with imp, page 65

complete without seam allowance

scarf 1 ×

fabric fold

hat

1 ×

full 1cm (½in) seam allowance

Sunday Breakfast in the Garden, page 22

Napkin, page 25

From the Heart, page 34

Gift tag, page 35

Everything in Its Place, page 8

Key holder, page 9

Bag pendant, page 11

Slippers, page 13

Sweet Dreams, page 46

Bookmark and coat hanger, page 49

A Cup of Coffee, Please!, page 38

Crockery, page 39

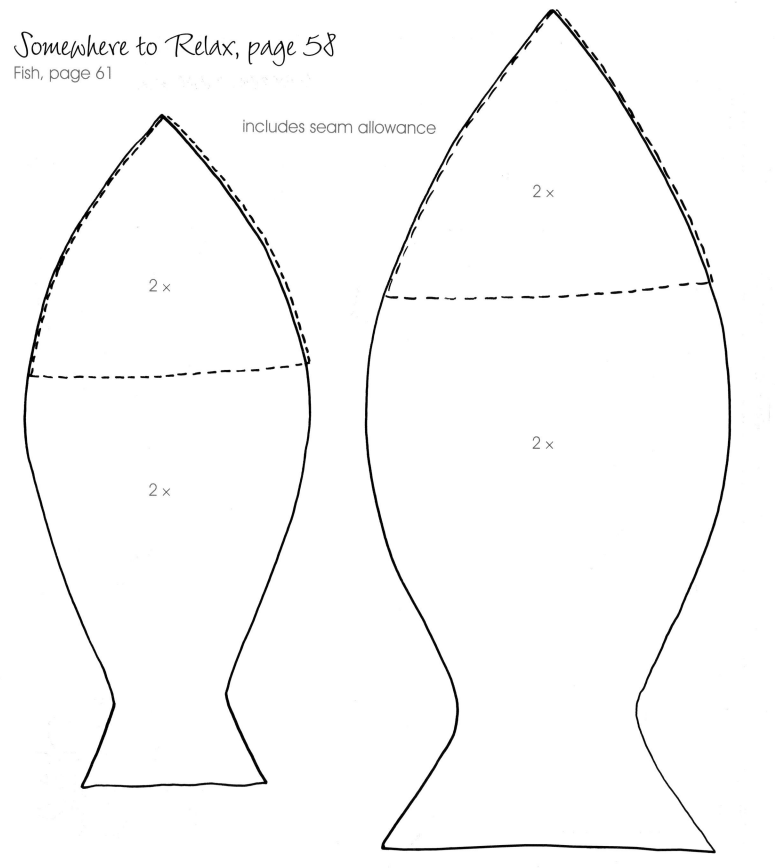

Somewhere to Relax, page 58

Fish, page 61

includes seam allowance

2×

2×

2×

2×

2×

Publishing information

First published in Great Britain 2010 by Search Press Limited,
Wellwood, North Farm Road, Tunbridge Wells, Kent TN2 3DR

Reprinted 2011

Original German edition published as Dekoträume aus Mittsommerland.

Copyright © 2009 frechverlag GmbH, Stuttgart, Germany (www.frech.de)

This edition published by arrangement with Claudia Böhme Rights & Literary Agency, Hannover, Germany (www.agency-boehme.com)

English translation by Cicero Translations

English edition edited and typeset by GreenGate Publishing Services

ISBN: 978-1-84448-603-8

We would like to thank the following companies: Gütermann creativ/KnorrPrandell (Gutach/Lichtenfels), Rayher Hobby GmbH (Laupheim), DECO-LINE, Kollnau, Veno (Bad Bentheim-Gildehaus), Freudenberg (Weinheim), IHR (Essen), Westfalenstoffe (Münster) for their kind support with materials.

ITEMS: Nadja Knab-Leers (pages 8–12, 14/15, 22–25, 36–41, 44–49, 52–55, 58–63), Heike Roland/Stefanie Thomas (pages 13, 16–19, 26–35, 50/51, 56/57, 64/65)
PHOTOS: frechverlag GmbH, 70499 Stuttgart; lichtpunkt, Michael Ruder, Stuttgart